YOU HAVE BEEN WARNED!

YOU HAVE BEEN WARNED!
Biblical Laws,
Warnings & Consequences
Synopsis

Penn Turner

YOU HAVE BEEN WARNED!
Biblical Laws, Warnings & Consequences
Synopsis
ISBN: 978-1-09369-191-7
Copyright © 2019 ~ All rights reserved.
1st Amendment Christian Exchange (1stACE) Publisher
Printed in the United States of America

YOU HAVE BEEN WARNED!
was revised from the following original Synopsis versions:

1. *Warnings & Consequences Synopsis (OT)*
   ISBN: 978-1-4675-4216-6 © Copyright 2012

2. *Warnings & Consequences Synopsis (NT)*
   ISBN: 978-1-4675-4217-3 © Copyright 2012

Cover designed by KDP Cover Designer.

Background picture from Bing Images Creative Commons
PROFESSORES LUSOS: Setembro 2010-http://3.bp.blogspot.com

DEDICATION

*This Synopsis is dedicated to the
'Body of Christ' and the 'Army of God'.
Always let the Holy Spirit be your guide.*

Table of Contents

Table of Contents

ADDENDUMS
  MISSION STATEMENT
  CONCLUSION
  PERSONAL NOTES

AUTHOR'S PREFACE

"My people are destroyed for lack of knowledge:..." Hosea 4:6

Greetings in the name of our Lord and Savior Jesus Christ.

Currently there exists an abundance of published resources on God's promises to His children. These promises are found printed on calendars, in books, and recorded on tapes. There are also books written on Biblical laws and warnings *but* this resource uses an unique format to present God's laws and warnings.

"YOU HAVE BEEN WARNED!" resource synopsis was designed to increase your awareness in God's Word so you can escape the possible consequences of an untimely death, loss of finances or have Christ deny you.

This resource identifies the Biblical laws and warnings with their punishing consequences that will occur *if one freely chooses to ignore God's laws* and not repent. Therefore, we must study and know His Word because, "Moreover by them is thy servant warned: ...." (Psalm 19:11)

It is agreeable that Christians are no longer under the 'Law of Moses' but the astute student of the Bible can confirm that many Old Testament warnings are repeated in the New Testament scriptures. In fact, the Old Testament was often referred to by Jesus Christ (i.e., Matthew 4:7 & Deuteronomy 6:16; Matthew 7:23 & Psalm 6:8).

Unfortunately, many readers will not accept this synopsis of Biblical laws and warnings *nonetheless* this synopsis had to be put it out there. Let the Holy Spirit be your guide.

Reader, you have been warned!

READER INFORMATION

In this synopsis the laws, warnings and consequences with their locations are given. This will allow you the opportunity to explore the Bible to confirm *and* learn the Word. There is space on each page for your notes and comments.

The '**Key**' at the top of each page explains the categories as:
- o **Warning:** chosen action, spoken word, thought or lifestyle contrary to God's & Jesus' commands, statutes & teachings
- o **Consequence:** for not heeding the law or warning
- o **Location:** in the Bible: book, chapter and verse(s)

Note that the majority of the verses are from the King James Version (KJV) of the Holy Bible. The additional Bible translations used in this synopsis were:
- o Modern English Version (MEV)
- o New King James Version (NKJV)
- o The Living Bible (TLB)
- o New International Version (NIV)
- o The Amplified Bible Classic Edition (AMPC)
- o New Revised Standard Version (NRSV)

The goal was to select the verse(s) from the Bible translation that provided the strongest interpretation of each law and warning.

To view multiple versions of the Bible at the same time go to Bible Gateway's website. Scroll down the home page to learn more about using their site.

OLD TESTAMENT

OLD TESTAMENT
A

Warning: chosen action, spoken word, thought or lifestyle contrary to God's & Jesus' commands, statutes & teachings	Consequence(s) for not heeding the law or warning	Location in the Bible: book, chapter and verse(s)
A false witness	Will Perish	Proverbs 21:28
A fool	Will Suffer Failure	Proverbs 10:10
A fool's wrath	Quickly And Openly Becomes Known	Proverbs 12:16 (AMPC)
A fool's vow	Offensive To God	Ecclesiastes 5:4 – 5
A high look and a proud heart	Sin In God's Eyes	Proverbs 21:4 (AMPC)
Adding to God's Word	God Will Reprimand You - Labeled As A Liar	Proverbs 30:5 - 6
Adultery	Destroys Your Soul	Proverbs 6:32 – 33
Adultery with neighbor's wife	Defiles Thyself With Her	Leviticus 18:20
Anyone that swears falsely by God's name	A Curse Takes Up Residence In Their Home	Zechariah 5:3 - 4

OLD TESTAMENT
B

Warning: chosen action, spoken word, thought or lifestyle contrary to God's & Jesus' commands, statutes & teachings	Consequence (s) for not heeding the law or warning	Location in the Bible: book, chapter and verse(s)
Backslide to serve strange gods	God Will Turn To Do You Hurt Then Consume You	Joshua 24:20
Backslider	Righteousness Not Remembered And Will Die	Ezekiel 18:24 (NIV)
Backslider	Remain In The Congregation Of The Spiritually Dead	Proverbs 21:16 (AMPC)
Bearing false witness	Mandatory Punishment To Put Away Evil – So, Do To Him As He Conspired To Have Done To The Accused	Deuteronomy 19:18 - 19
Blasphemy	Shall Be Put To Death	Leviticus 24:15 - 16
Bless yourself in your heart for protection after turning from God	Curses Fall Upon You *And* Name Blotted Out From Under Heaven	Deuteronomy 29:18 – 20
Bloody & deceitful people	Shall Not Live Out Their Full Days On Earth	Psalm 55:23
Body language of a wicked person	His Fate Is Sudden Calamity	Proverbs 6:12 – 15 (MEV)
Break God's commands & statues regarding '*immoral relationships*'	Land Will Vomit Out Its Inhabitants – People And Land Become Defiled	Leviticus 18:3 – 29 (AMPC)
Breaking God's covenant	Offender Shall Be Cut Off From His People	Genesis 17:14

OLD TESTAMENT
C

Warning: chosen action, spoken word, thought or lifestyle contrary to God's & Jesus' commands, statutes & teachings	Consequence (s) for not heeding the law or warning	Location in the Bible: book, chapter and verse(s)
Careless use of God's name	Guilty And Held Accountable	Deuteronomy 5:11
Choose to go after other gods	Person Becomes Cursed	Deuteronomy 11:26 - 28
Co-signing for others	Unnecessary Suffering And Disappointment	Proverbs 11:15 (AMPC) Proverbs 22:26 - 27 (AMPC)
Commit any one of the seven things the Lord hates	Abominations To The Lord	Proverbs 6:16 - 19
Contend with a fool	No Peace In Your Life	Proverbs 29:9
Create likeness of anything in heaven, on the earth or in the waters to worship	Sins Of The Father Passes To His Children Until Third and Fourth Generation	Exodus 20:4 - 5
Crooked judge	A Bribe Blinds And Corrupts The Judgement	Deuteronomy 16:19 (MEV)
Crooked merchant with assorted weights and measures	Abomination To The Lord	Proverbs 20:10 (AMPC) Proverbs 20: 23 (MEV)
Cross-gender dressing	Abomination To The Lord Thy God	Deuteronomy 22:5
Curses parent	Child's Lamp Shall Be Put Out In Obscure Darkness	Proverbs 20:20

OLD TESTAMENT
D

Warning: chosen action, spoken word, thought or lifestyle contrary to God's & Jesus' commands, statutes & teachings	Consequence (s) for not heeding the law or warning	Location in the Bible: book, chapter and verse(s)
Deceitful heart & vicious tongue	A Sorrowful Life Full Of Mischief	Proverbs 17:20 (MEV)
Deceitfully gained inheritance	Inheritance Will Not Be Blessed	Proverbs 20:21 (AMPC)
Deceived by heart to worship other gods	God's Wrath Kindled Against You	Deuteronomy 11:16 - 17
Defiance to God's laws	Cursed Through Your Sins	Deuteronomy 27:15 – 26
Deliberate eavesdropping	Hurt By The Words Of Others	Ecclesiastes 7:21 - 22
Despise & reject the Word of the Lord	Guilty And Shall Be Utterly Cut Off	Numbers 15:30 - 31 (AMPC)
Despisers of God's commandments	Will Be Rebuked By God	Proverbs 19:16 (NKJV)
Dishonest rich men & women	Will Be Remembered As A Broke Fool	Jeremiah 17:11 (MEV)
Dishonor your parent(s)	Days On Earth Are Made Short	Exodus 20:12
Dismisses correction from God	Person Goes Astray	Proverbs 10:17 (NKJV)
Disobedience	People Will Perish Without Knowledge	Job 36:12

OLD TESTAMENT
D

Warning: chosen action, spoken word, thought or lifestyle contrary to God's & Jesus' commands, statutes & teachings	Consequence (s) for not heeding the law or warning	Location in the Bible: book, chapter and verse(s)
Disobedience & carelessness by a man of God	Easily Tricked Into Disobedience – Suffer A Vicious Death	1 Kings 13:8 – 26
Disobedient & rebellious	Hand Of The Lord Will Be Against You	1 Samuel 12:15
Disobey God's commandment	Will Suffer God's Reprimand	Genesis 2:17
Divorce because of your infidelity	God Will No Longer Regard Your Offerings	Malachi 2:13 – 16 (NIV)
Does not observe God's commandments nor statutes	Overtaken By Curses In All Aspects Of Your Life	Deuteronomy 28:15 - 66
Doing evil	No Remembrance Of Your Existence	Psalm 34:16
Drunkards	Bondage - Eyes Will Observe Strange Things - Their Minds Have Perverse Thoughts	Proverbs 23:29 - 35 (AMPC)
Drunkards & gluttons	Stricken With Poverty	Proverbs 23:21

OLD TESTAMENT
E

Warning: chosen action, spoken word, thought or lifestyle contrary to God's & Jesus' commands, statutes & teachings	Consequence (s) for not heeding the law or warning	Location in the Bible: book, chapter and verse(s)
Enticing relative, spouse, or friend to serve other gods	Death To Anyone Attempting To Turn Someone From God	Deuteronomy 13:6 – 10 (MEV)
Evil doers & liars	Evil Associates With Evil And Liars Band With Other Liars	Proverbs 17:4 (NKJV)

OLD TESTAMENT
F

Warning: chosen action, spoken word, thought or lifestyle contrary to God's & Jesus' commands, statutes & teachings	Consequence (s) for not heeding the law or warning	Location in the Bible: book, chapter and verse(s)
Fail to warn the wicked	Held Accountable For The Wicked Man Or Woman Dying In His Or Her Sin(s)	Ezekiel 3:18
Faith in own riches	Person Will Fall	Proverbs 11:28
False prophets & dreamer of dreams	Grave Punishment To Anyone Attempting To Turn People From God	Deuteronomy 13:1 – 5

OLD TESTAMENT
F

Warning: chosen action, spoken word, thought or lifestyle contrary to God's & Jesus' commands, statutes & teachings	Consequence (s) for not heeding the law or warning	Location in the Bible: book, chapter and verse(s)
False witness & a liar	Will Not Escape Punishment	Deuteronomy 19:18 - 20 Proverbs 19:5, 9 Proverbs 19:28 – 29
Falsely accuse an employee or servant before their employer or master	Accuser Becomes Cursed And Guilty Of Adding To The Problems Of The Worker	Proverbs 30:10 (AMPC)
father allows sin into his house	Judgment Comes Upon his Household	1 Samuel 3:12 – 14
Flattering lips & proud workers of iniquity (wickedness)	The Lord Will Not Deal Gently With Them	Psalm 12:2 – 4
Following after an immoral woman	Remorse - Lost Years - Body Riddled With Disease - Loss Of Wealth - Life Shorten	Proverbs 5:6 - 12 (AMPC)
Following after prostitutes & strange women	Untimely Death	Proverbs 2:18 - 19
Following after unproductive people	Stricken With Poverty	Proverbs 28:19

OLD TESTAMENT
F

Warning: chosen action, spoken word, thought or lifestyle contrary to God's & Jesus' commands, statutes & teachings	Consequence (s) for not heeding the law or warning	Location in the Bible: book, chapter and verse(s)
Foolish existence	Perverted Lifestyle - Your Heart Becomes Resentful Against The Lord	Proverbs 19:3 (AMPC)
Foolishly believe that past righteous deeds will cover current sins	Lost Because Of Renewed Sinning	Ezekiel 33:12 – 13 Ezekiel 33:18 (MEV)
Forgetting the LORD your God	You Shall Surely Perish	Deuteronomy 8:19 – 20 (MEV)
Forgetting to keep your soul diligent	God's Wonders Depart From Your Heart And Mind Then Eventually Your Life	Deuteronomy 4:9 (AMPC)
Forsake God's laws	God Will Not Spare The Rod On Disobedient Children	Psalm 89:30 – 32
Forsake God's statutes & commandments	Casted Out Of God's Sight - Country Punished	2 Chronicles 7:19 - 22
Full of pride & a conceited spirit	Humiliated Life And Personal Destruction	Proverbs 16:18

OLD TESTAMENT
G

Warning: chosen action, spoken word, thought or lifestyle contrary to God's & Jesus' commands, statutes & teachings	Consequence (s) for not heeding the law or warning	Location in the Bible: book, chapter and verse(s)
Genetic seed engineering	Defiled Yield	Deuteronomy 22:9 (NKJV)
Greedy unfair business men & women	Will Lose Their Fortunes To The Poor	Proverbs 28:8 (AMPC)

OLD TESTAMENT
H

Warning: chosen action, spoken word, thought or lifestyle contrary to God's & Jesus' commands, statutes & teachings	Consequence (s) for not heeding the law or warning	Location in the Bible: book, chapter and verse(s)
Hasten to be rich	Stricken With Poverty	Proverbs 28:21 - 22 (MEV)
Haters of God	God Will Repay You Face To Face	Deuteronomy 7:10 (NKJV)
Haters of God's knowledge	God Will Not Answer Their Call For Help	Proverbs 1:27 – 32

OLD TESTAMENT
H

Warning: chosen action, spoken word, thought or lifestyle contrary to God's & Jesus' commands, statutes & teachings	Consequence (s) for not heeding the law or warning	Location in the Bible: book, chapter and verse(s)
Have no fear of God	Tragic Results In Your Life	Proverbs 1:27 – 32
Having angry associates	Your Soul Is Captured By Learning Their Ways	Proverbs 22:24 – 25
Heart departs from the Lord	Shall Not Be Able To See Good When It Comes	Jeremiah 17:5 – 6 (MEV)
Heart turns from God	LORD Thy God Will Denounce You - You Shall Surely Perish	Deuteronomy 30:17 - 19
Homosexuality	An Abomination To God Your Father	Leviticus 18:22

OLD TESTAMENT

I

Warning: chosen action, spoken word, thought or lifestyle contrary to God's & Jesus' commands, statutes & teachings	Consequence (s) for not heeding the law or warning	Location in the Bible: book, chapter and verse(s)
Idolatry sacrifice	Person Will Be Utterly Destroyed	Exodus 22:20 (MEV)
Ignore continuously God's corrections & remain obstinate	Sudden Destruction For That Person	Proverbs 29:1
Ignores the poor	Will Have Many Curses In Their Life	Proverbs 28:27
Immoral woman	Final Destination Is Hell	Proverbs 5:3 – 6 (MEV)
Influence others with lies	Downfall Of Their Government	Proverbs 29:12 (NIV)
Inquisitive about gods of other religions	Ensnared Into Following Them	Deuteronomy 12:30
Involvement with a false matter	God Will Not Justify The Wicked	Exodus 23:7

OLD TESTAMENT
J

Warning: chosen action, spoken word, thought or lifestyle contrary to God's & Jesus' commands, statutes & teachings	Consequence (s) for not heeding the law or warning	Location in the Bible: book, chapter and verse(s)
Justifier of the wicked & condemner of the innocent	Both Of Them Become Abominations To The LORD	Proverbs 17:15
Justifies the wicked as righteous & innocent	Cursed By The People And Abhorred By Nations	Proverbs 24:24

OLD TESTAMENT
K

Warning: chosen action, spoken word, thought or lifestyle contrary to God's & Jesus' commands, statutes & teachings	Consequence (s) for not heeding the law or warning	Location in the Bible: book, chapter and verse(s)
Keep a cursed graven image in home	You Will Become Cursed Like It	Deuteronomy 7:25 – 26
Kidnap for slavery	Kidnapper Surely Put To Death	Exodus 21:16 (TLB)

OLD TESTAMENT
L

Warning: chosen action, spoken word, thought or lifestyle contrary to God's & Jesus' commands, statutes & teachings	Consequence (s) for not heeding the law or warning	Location in the Bible: book, chapter and verse(s)
Leaders under the influence	Unsteady Government	Proverbs 31:3 – 5 (NIV)
Liars & wicked doers	Will Not Stay In God's Presence	Psalm 101:7 - 8 (MEV)
Live to party	Will Always Be Poor	Proverbs 21:17 (MEV)
Loathe God's commandments & judgments	God's Wrath Released In All Areas Of Your Life	Leviticus 26:14 – 39 (MEV)
Lying to obtain riches	Dishonest Gains Will Never Last	Proverbs 21:6 (NIV)

OLD TESTAMENT
M

Warning: chosen action, spoken word, thought or lifestyle contrary to God's & Jesus' commands, statutes & teachings	Consequence (s) for not heeding the law or warning	Location in the Bible: book, chapter and verse(s)
Make haste after another god	Your Sorrows Will Be Multiplied	Psalm 16:4 (MEV)
Making a rash vow	Will Later Reconsider The Vow	Proverbs 20:25 (NIV)
Man not in favor with God makes an easy prey	Easily Snared By A Prostitute's Mouth	Proverbs 22:14 (MEV)

Warning: chosen action, spoken word, thought or lifestyle contrary to God's & Jesus' commands, statutes & teachings	Consequence (s) for not heeding the law or warning	Location in the Bible: book, chapter and verse(s)
Man or woman trusting in their own works	Work Is Done In Vain – Life Full Of Anxiety	Psalm 127:1-2 (MEV)
Men & women that put trust in another person	Cursed And No Hope For Their Future	Jeremiah 17:5 – 6 (TLB)
Merchants with dishonest weights	Short Life - An Abomination Before The LORD	Deuteronomy 25:13 - 16 (MEV)
Mocker of enemy's misfortune	The Lord Turns His Wrath Away From Your Enemy To You	Proverbs 24:17 - 18 (MEV)
Mockers of the poor & gloaters over another's disaster	They Will Be Punished By The Creator	Proverbs 17:5 (NIV)
Money given to the Lord's house *after* an immoral act performed by a whore or sodomite	Both Acts Are An Abomination To the Lord And Their Money	Deuteronomy 23:18
Mouth of a foolish bragger	Chance Of Appearing Foolish In Public	Proverbs 27:1
Murder	Murderer Will Be Put To Death	Genesis 9:6 Exodus 21:12, 14 Leviticus 24:17

OLD TESTAMENT
N

Warning: chosen action, spoken word, thought or lifestyle contrary to God's & Jesus' commands, statutes & teachings	Consequence (s) for not heeding the law or warning	Location in the Bible: book, chapter and verse(s)
Neglect keeping God's commandments, judgments & statues	Your Pride Replaced God	Deuteronomy 8:11 – 14
No chastisement given to a person always consumed with anger	Person Feels Free To Be A Repetitive Offender	Proverbs 19:19 (AMPC)
No respect for God's Son	Person Shall Perish	Psalm 2:12 (AMPC)
Not warning the backslider	Held Accountable For Backslider Dying In Sin	Ezekiel 3:20

OLD TESTAMENT
O

Warning: chosen action, spoken word, thought or lifestyle contrary to God's & Jesus' commands, statutes & teachings	Consequence (s) for not heeding the law or warning	Location in the Bible: book, chapter and verse(s)
One that ignores the cries of the poor	When Their Suffering Comes No One Will Hear Their Cry	Proverbs 21:13
Oppressing your employee	You Are Guilty And Held Accountable	Deuteronomy 24:14 - 15
Oppression of widows & fatherless children	God Will Hear Their Cries Then Kills The Oppressor	Exodus 22:22 – 24
Oppressors of the poor & givers to the rich	Both Will Come To Poverty	Proverbs 22:16

OLD TESTAMENT
P

Warning: chosen action, spoken word, thought or lifestyle contrary to God's & Jesus' commands, statutes & teachings	Consequence (s) for not heeding the law or warning	Location in the Bible: book, chapter and verse(s)
Partner of a thief	Falls Under A Curse	Proverbs 29:24 (AMPC)
Passover not observed	Person Is Cut Off From The People And Bears Their Sin	Numbers 9:13
Pastors that destroys, scatters, drives away, & do not visit God's flock	God Will Visit Upon Them The Evil Of Their Deeds	Jeremiah 23: 1 – 2
People that do not punish a person sacrificing a child to a false god	God Sets His Face Against Them, Their Family And Cut Them All Off From The People	Leviticus 20:4 – 5 (AMPC)
People that reverse good & evil	Woe Unto Them	Isaiah 5:20 - 23
People that secretly hate	Their Wickedness Shall Be Revealed Before Everyone	Proverbs 26: 24 – 26
Perverse heart	Can't Be In God's Presence	Psalm 101:3 – 4
Plotters against the just	Lord *Laughs* At Them	Psalm 37:12 – 13
Power of the tongue	Can Determine Life And Death	Proverbs 18:21

OLD TESTAMENT
P

Warning: chosen action, spoken word, thought or lifestyle contrary to God's & Jesus' commands, statutes & teachings	Consequence (s) for not heeding the law or warning	Location in the Bible: book, chapter and verse(s)
Practice bestiality	Person Was Put To Death Along With The Beast	Leviticus 20:15 – 16
Practice homosexuality	An Abomination Before God	Leviticus 20:13
Practicing medium, necromancer, or wizard	They Will Initiate Their Own Doom	Leviticus 20:27 (MEV)
Premature response before hearing all the facts	Incurs Public Embarrassment	Proverbs 18:13
Priests & other religious leaders that will not hear *nor* give glory to the Lord's name	God Will Send You A Curse – He Will Curse Your Blessings - Corrupt Your Seed - *And* Spread Dung Upon Your Face	Malachi 2:2 – 3
Prostitute your daughters	Land Becomes Wicked	Leviticus 19:29
Proud heart	Abomination To The Lord - Person Will Be Punished	Proverbs 16:5
Provoke God to anger	Person Will Suddenly Perish	Deuteronomy 4:25 - 26
Purposely ignore God's prophets	Held Accountable To The Lord	Deuteronomy 18:18 - 19
Purposely not hearing God's law	Your Prayers Shall Be An Abomination	Proverbs 28:9

OLD TESTAMENT
R

Warning: chosen action, spoken word, thought or lifestyle contrary to God's & Jesus' commands, statutes & teachings	Consequence (s) for not heeding the law or warning	Location in the Bible: book, chapter and verse(s)
Refuse to testify for justice	You Shall Bear Your Iniquity (Sin)	Leviticus 5:1 (TLB)
Rewards evil for good	Evil Will Not Depart From Your House	Proverbs 17:13
Riotous living	Lose Devine Understanding	Hosea 4:11 (AMPC)
Rob God with tithes & offerings	Cursed With A Curse	Malachi 3:8 – 9
Rob the poor & oppress the afflicted	Lord Will Punish Them	Proverbs 22:22 - 23

OLD TESTAMENT
S

Warning: chosen action, spoken word, thought or lifestyle contrary to God's & Jesus' commands, statutes & teachings	Consequence (s) for not heeding the law or warning	Location in the Bible: book, chapter and verse(s)
Sacrifice of the wicked	Abomination To The Lord	Proverbs 21:27
Seeking out fortune tellers & wizards for guidance	Will Become Defiled By Association	Leviticus 19:31

OLD TESTAMENT
S

Warning: chosen action, spoken word, thought or lifestyle contrary to God's & Jesus' commands, statutes & teachings	Consequence (s) for not heeding the law or warning	Location in the Bible: book, chapter and verse(s)
Self-confident mouth of a fool	Life Full Of Contention - Invites A [Good] Beating - Self-Destruct	Proverbs 18:6 - 7 (AMPC)
Sex with animals	Causes Confusion And Perversion	Leviticus 18:23 (AMPC)
Sinners	Tormented During The Great Day Of The LORD	Zephaniah 1:14 - 18
Sleep with uncle's wife or brother's wife	Shall Be Childless	Leviticus 20:20 - 21
Slow to keep a vow to the Lord	Committed A Sin And God Expects You To Pay	Deuteronomy 23:21
Sows iniquity	Reap Catastrophe	Proverbs 22:8 (AMPC)

OLD TESTAMENT
T

Warning: chosen action, spoken word, thought or lifestyle contrary to God's & Jesus' commands, statutes & teachings	Consequence (s) for not heeding the law or warning	Location in the Bible: book, chapter and verse(s)
Taking God's silence as a green light to sin	God Tears The Wicked To Pieces	Psalm 50:16 - 22 (AMPC)
Thieves & anyone that swears falsely by God's name	Moving Evil Will Consume Their Home	Zechariah 5:3 - 4 (MEV)
Those who cause the righteous to go astray	Eventually Fall Into Their Own Trap	Proverbs 28:10

OLD TESTAMENT
U

Warning: chosen action, spoken word, thought or lifestyle contrary to God's & Jesus' commands, statutes & teachings	Consequence (s) for not heeding the law or warning	Location in the Bible: book, chapter and verse(s)
Using God's name in vain	Guilty And Will Be Punished	Exodus 20:7 (AMPC)

OLD TESTAMENT
V

Warning: chosen action, spoken word, thought or lifestyle contrary to God's & Jesus' commands, statutes & teachings	Consequence (s) for not heeding the law or warning	Location in the Bible: book, chapter and verse(s)
Visiting busybodies	People Hate To See You Coming - Cause Neighbor(s) To Hate	Proverbs 25:17

OLD TESTAMENT
W

Warning: chosen action, spoken word, thought or lifestyle contrary to God's & Jesus' commands, statutes & teachings	Consequence (s) for not heeding the law or warning	Location in the Bible: book, chapter and verse(s)
Whoring after familiar spirits & wizards	Offender Shall Be Cut Off	Leviticus 20:6
Worship other gods	Anger Of God Kindled Against You	Deuteronomy 6:14 – 15 (TLB)

NEW TESTAMENT

NEW TESTAMENT
A

Warning: chosen action, spoken word, thought or lifestyle contrary to God's & Jesus' commands, statutes & teachings	Consequence (s) for not heeding the law or warning	Location in the Bible: book, chapter and verse(s)
Any man who add to the words of the prophecy	God Will Add To That Person The Plagues Written In Revelation	Revelation 22:18 (NRSV)
Any man who eliminate words from this book of prophecy	God Will Take Away That Person's Part In Three Areas	Revelation 22:19 (MEV)
Anyone ashamed of Christ and His Word	Christ Shall Be Ashamed Of You	Mark 8:38
Anyone who worships the beast, his image *and* receives the beast's mark in their forehead or right hand	Shall Drink Of The Wine Of The Wrath Of God - Tormented With Fire And Brimstone	Revelation 14:9 - 11
Apostasy (open spiritual rebellion, abandoning faith in Jesus Christ)	Nails The Son Of God To The Cross Again By Rejecting Him – Holds Christ Up To Public Mocking And Shame	Hebrews 6:4 – 8 (MEV)

NEW TESTAMENT
B

Warning: chosen action, spoken word, thought or lifestyle contrary to God's & Jesus' commands, statutes & teachings	Consequence (s) for not heeding the law or warning	Location in the Bible: book, chapter and verse(s)
Backsliders	Return To A Worse State Of Sin	**2 P**eter 2:20 – 22 (MEV)
Blasphemy against the Holy Ghost	No Forgiveness	Matthew 12:31- 32 **M**ark 3:29
Blind leading the blind	Both Will Spiritual Fall	Matthew 15:14
Body (house) still not occupied with the Holy Spirit	Unclean spirit Returns With Others To Repossess The Body	Matthew 12:43 - 45 (NKJV)

NEW TESTAMENT
C

Warning: chosen action, spoken word, thought or lifestyle contrary to God's & Jesus' commands, statutes & teachings	Consequence (s) for not heeding the law or warning	Location in the Bible: book, chapter and verse(s)
Call a brother a fool	Will Be In Danger Of Hell Fire	Matthew 5:22 (AMPC)
Choose not to repent *or* become child-like	Will Not Enter Heaven	Matthew 18:3 (AMPC)
Christians committing fornication	Sinned Against Own Body	**1** Corinthians 6:15 - 20 (TLB)

NEW TESTAMENT
C

Warning: chosen action, spoken word, thought or lifestyle contrary to God's & Jesus' commands, statutes & teachings	Consequence (s) for not heeding the law or warning	Location in the Bible: book, chapter and verse(s)
Christians who willfully sin	Judgment Then Hell	Hebrews 10:26 - 29 (NIV)
Church leaders that forgot Christ's warning	Savage Wolves Enters Into Their Congregations	Acts 20:28 – 32
Covetous people	Start World Wars And Conflicts - Their Prayers Will Go Unanswered	James 4:1 - 4 (TLB)
Crafty self-proclaimed wise men & women	God Uses Man's Worldly Wisdom To Trap Them	1 Corinthians 3:19 (TLB)

NEW TESTAMENT
D

Warning: chosen action, spoken word, thought or lifestyle contrary to God's & Jesus' commands, statutes & teachings	Consequence (s) for not heeding the law or warning	Location in the Bible: book, chapter and verse(s)
Defilers of their temple (body)	God Will Destroy That Person	1 Corinthians 3:16 - 17
Deny Christ	Denied By Christ	Luke 12:9 2 Timothy 2:12

NEW TESTAMENT
D

Warning: chosen action, spoken word, thought or lifestyle contrary to God's & Jesus' commands, statutes & teachings	Consequence (s) for not heeding the law or warning	Location in the Bible: book, chapter and verse(s)
Depart from God	Heart Becomes Hardened By Sin	Hebrews 3:12 – 13 (NKJV)
Dishonor parents	Life Will Not Go Well - A Short Life	Ephesians 6:1 - 3
Disobedient	Deceived By Futile Words To Sin - Will Suffer The Wrath Of God	Ephesians 5:6 - 7

NEW TESTAMENT
E

Warning: chosen action, spoken word, thought or lifestyle contrary to God's & Jesus' commands, statutes & teachings	Consequence (s) for not heeding the law or warning	Location in the Bible: book, chapter and verse(s)
End-time mockers	Void Of The Holy Spirit - Walking In Their Own Lusts	Jude 17 - 19 (NRSV)
Every person that rejects truth & follow evil	Troubled Life And Full Of Distress	Romans 2:8 - 9

NEW TESTAMENT
F

Warning: chosen action, spoken word, thought or lifestyle contrary to God's & Jesus' commands, statutes & teachings	Consequence (s) for not heeding the law or warning	Location in the Bible: book, chapter and verse(s)
Fail to be on guard	Easily Led Away By The Deception Of The Wicked	**2 P**eter 3:17 (MEV)
Followers of Christ	Hated And Many Will Be Killed	**M**atthew 24:9
Followers of Christ	Hated And Betrayed By Family – Possibly Murdered	Luke 21:16 - 17
Followers of Christ	World Will Hate And Persecute You	John 15:18 - 23

NEW TESTAMENT
H

Warning: chosen action, spoken word, thought or lifestyle contrary to God's & Jesus' commands, statutes & teachings	Consequence (s) for not heeding the law or warning	Location in the Bible: book, chapter and verse(s)
Having an unforgiving heart	God Will Not Forgive You	**M**atthew 6:15 (AMPC)
Hold anger against a brother	In Danger Of Hell Fire	**M**atthew 5:22 (AMPC)

NEW TESTAMENT
I

Warning: chosen action, spoken word, thought or lifestyle contrary to God's & Jesus' commands, statutes & teachings	Consequence (s) for not heeding the law or warning	Location in the Bible: book, chapter and verse(s)
Ignore the warnings from Israel's history	Will Repeat Their Evils – Will Also Displease God – Suffer Their Punishments	1 Corinthians 10:5 – 13 (NIV)
Insensitive dad	Produce Negative Children	Colossians 3:21 (TLB)
Insufficient provider for family	Worthless Person - Worse Than An Unbeliever	1 Timothy 5:8
Irreverence the Holy Ghost	Never Forgiven	Luke 12:10
Irreverently take Holy Communion	Profane The Body And Blood Of Christ - Eat And Drink Damnation	1 Corinthians 11:24 - 31 (MEV)

NEW TESTAMENT
J

Warning: chosen action, spoken word, thought or lifestyle contrary to God's & Jesus' commands, statutes & teachings	Consequence (s) for not heeding the law or warning	Location in the Bible: book, chapter and verse(s)
Judging others	Judged Later By Your Own Measures - Will Condemn Self	Matthew 7:1 - 2 (AMPC) Romans 2:1

NEW TESTAMENT
K

Warning: chosen action, spoken word, thought or lifestyle contrary to God's & Jesus' commands, statutes & teachings	Consequence (s) for not heeding the law or warning	Location in the Bible: book, chapter and verse(s)
Killers	Answerable To Judgment	Matthew 5:21

NEW TESTAMENT
L

Warning: chosen action, spoken word, thought or lifestyle contrary to God's & Jesus' commands, statutes & teachings	Consequence (s) for not heeding the law or warning	Location in the Bible: book, chapter and verse(s)
Lack control of your tongue	Your Religion Is Worthless	James 1:26
Lovers of money	Root Of All Types Of Evil – They Wonder Away From The Faith	1 Timothy 6:10
Lust in your heart	Guilty Of Adultery	Matthew 5:28

NEW TESTAMENT
M

Warning: chosen action, spoken word, thought or lifestyle contrary to God's & Jesus' commands, statutes & teachings	Consequence (s) for not heeding the law or warning	Location in the Bible: book, chapter and verse(s)
Man or woman who bring the temptation to sin	Life Full Of Woe	Matthew 18:7 (AMPC) Luke 17:1
Men and women who continually refuse God's truth regarding salvation	Eventually Receives A Strong Delusion	2 Thessalonians 2:9 – 12 (TLB)
Misinterpret Scripture for personal gratification	The Distortion Of The Word By The Wicked Leads Unknowledgeable People Astray - Personal Destruction	2 Peter 3:15 – 18 (MEV)

NEW TESTAMENT
O

Warning: chosen action, spoken word, thought or lifestyle contrary to God's & Jesus' commands, statutes & teachings	Consequence (s) for not heeding the law or warning	Location in the Bible: book, chapter and verse(s)
Observer(s) of the 'Old Law'	Remain Under The Old Testament (OT) Curses	Galatians 3:10 – 12 (TLB)

NEW TESTAMENT
P

Warning: chosen action, spoken word, thought or lifestyle contrary to God's & Jesus' commands, statutes & teachings	Consequence (s) for not heeding the law or warning	Location in the Bible: book, chapter and verse(s)
Partaking in Holy Communion while unworthy and without discernment of its true meaning	Can Become Unhealthy - Some Will Die – Secure Damnation	1 Corinthians 11:27 - 31 (MEV)
People living to please their desires	Reap What Is Sown To The Flesh	Galatians 6:7 – 8 (NIV)
Performing good deeds publicly	No Reward From The Father	Matthew 6:1 - 2 (NIV)
Person who shows no mercy to others	Will Have Judgment Without Mercy	James 2:13
Preaching contrary to Christ's gospel	Fall Under God's Curses	Galatians 1:8- 10 (MEV)
Publicly deny Christ	Christ Will Deny You Before His Father	Matthew 10:33

NEW TESTAMENT
R

Warning: chosen action, spoken word, thought or lifestyle contrary to God's & Jesus' commands, statutes & teachings	Consequence (s) for not heeding the law or warning	Location in the Bible: book, chapter and verse(s)
Rebellious against the ruling civil government	Punishment Will Follow - Bring Down Judgment Upon Yourself And Comrades	Romans 13:1 – 7 (MEV)
Refuse to humble self like a child to receive heaven	Not Allowed To Enter Heaven	Mark 10:15 (AMPC) Luke 18:16 - 17 (AMPC)
Reject Christ and His Teachings	Judgement By The Words Of Christ	John 12:48 (AMPC)

NEW TESTAMENT
S

Warning: chosen action, spoken word, thought or lifestyle contrary to God's & Jesus' commands, statutes & teachings	Consequence (s) for not heeding the law or warning	Location in the Bible: book, chapter and verse(s)
Scoffers	All The Prophets' Warnings Will Come Upon You	Acts 13:40 – 41 (AMPC)
Servers of self & ignores the needy	Everlasting Punishment	Matthew 25:41 - 46

NEW TESTAMENT
S

Warning: chosen action, spoken word, thought or lifestyle contrary to God's & Jesus' commands, statutes & teachings	Consequence (s) for not heeding the law or warning	Location in the Bible: book, chapter and verse(s)
Speaker of blasphemous useless talk	Increase In Ungodliness	**2** Timothy 2:16
Spoken words are judged	Your Words Decide Your Eternity	**Matthew** 12:36 – 37 (MEV)

NEW TESTAMENT
T

Warning: chosen action, spoken word, thought or lifestyle contrary to God's & Jesus' commands, statutes & teachings	Consequence (s) for not heeding the law or warning	Location in the Bible: book, chapter and verse(s)
The unrighteous	Shall Not Inherit The Kingdom Of God	**1** Corinthians 6:8 – 10 (AMPC)
Transgressors from the doctrine of Christ	Does Not Have God - Cause Believers To Lose All Their Heavenly Rewards	**2** John 1:7 – 11 (MEV)
Trying to find favor with God by being circumcised	Christ Is Useless To You	**Galatians** 5:3 – 5 (TLB)

NEW TESTAMENT
U

Warning: chosen action, spoken word, thought or lifestyle contrary to God's & Jesus' commands, statutes & teachings	Consequence (s) for not heeding the law or warning	Location in the Bible: book, chapter and verse(s)
Uncultivated tongue	Defiles Whole Body - Possessed by a restless evil that is full of deadly poison	James 3:5 - 10 (NIV)

NEW TESTAMENT
V

Warning: chosen action, spoken word, thought or lifestyle contrary to God's & Jesus' commands, statutes & teachings	Consequence (s) for not heeding the law or warning	Location in the Bible: book, chapter and verse(s)
Violate any part of the Old Testament 'Law'	Guilty Of Breaking All Of The Law And Now A Lawbreaker	James 2:10 - 11 (NIV)

NEW TESTAMENT
W

Warning: chosen action, spoken word, thought or lifestyle contrary to God's & Jesus' commands, statutes & teachings	Consequence (s) for not heeding the law or warning	Location in the Bible: book, chapter and verse(s)
Watchers & members in Christ's church *fail* to turn away from church leaders in opposition of Christ's doctrine	Allows Division *AND* Hindrances Among The Brethren – The Weak And Simple Minded Are Easily Fooled	Romans 16:17 - 18 (AMPC)
Whoremongers, the unclean, covetous people and idolaters	No Inheritance In The Kingdom Of Christ And Of God	Ephesians 5:5
Wicked practice of swearing oaths	Fall Into Condemnation	James 5:12 (NIV)
Wonder from church to church	Cannot Endure Sound Doctrine - Accumulate Pastors' Teachings That Is Pleasing To Their Ears - Accept Teachings Based On Fables And Illusions	2 Timothy 4:2 - 4 (AMPC)
Workers of iniquity	Shut Out Of Heaven	Luke 13:25 – 28 (MEV)
Works of the flesh	Transgressor Of Any One Of The Works (of the flesh) Shall Not Inherit The Kingdom Of God	Galatians 5:19 – 21 (MEV)

ADDENDUMS

MISSION STATEMENT

"Jesus answered and said unto them, Ye do err, not knowing the scriptures, nor the power of God." Matthew 22:29

1st Amendment Christian Exchange (1stACE) was established under the guidance of the Holy Spirit to render an informative awareness of the Word.

Please understand that 1stACE only directs individuals to answers from the Holy Bible and Christian ministries.

The individual must come to their own decision.

1stACE acknowledges that Jesus Christ is Lord and the Son of God who died for our sins and rose again. Jesus conquered death and hell and is *now* sitting at the right hand of the Father.

1stACE believe that Jesus Christ will soon return as King of kings and Lord of lords!

Please pray for us according to Colossians 1:9-14 and Ephesians 6:19.

CONCLUSION

Thank you for purchasing *You Have Been Warned!*

We at 1ˢᵗ ACE designed this synopsis to be a well-informed resource that initiates an awareness of the laws and warnings from the Word.

We encourage you to confirm the Bible verses and their consequences in this synopsis. "Don't let others spoil your faith and joy with their philosophies, their wrong and shallow answers built on men's thoughts and ideas, instead of on what Christ has said." (Colossians 2:8 TLB)

May all our writings be a blessing to you in Jesus' Name.

Believers –
Study the Word! Believe the Word! Stand on the Word!
Wait patiently on the Lord.
Take heed that we ('The Body of Christ') *do not* have to
fight our God's battles because He lives.
He will act in His Own time and in His Own way.

Penn Turner

PERSONAL NOTES

PERSONAL NOTES

www.ingramcontent.com/pod-product-compliance
Lightning Source LLC
Chambersburg PA
CBHW081604280526
45788CB00011B/3544